SALLY BUXMAN

Top Shots

Foundational Visual Elements in Filmmaking

Contents

1

Chapter One - Introduction

Alfred Hitchcock once said, "If it's a good movie, the sound could go off and the audience would still have a pretty clear idea of what was going on". This really encapsulates what is so important about the visual techniques of a film. Whether your dream is to make the next summer blockbuster, to make the critics swoon over your unique vision, or if you just love movies and want to understand what goes into making them, there are essential visual tools in a filmmaker's tool belt that are tried and true elements found in all movies, and which are intrinsic to the telling of story on screen.

In this book we'll focus on the visual elements, the film photography basics, including the shot, the angle of a shot, light and dark and finally we'll touch on color. One could likely fill a full-length book covering these topics, but the goal here is to give you a brief introduction to these elements so that you appreciate what turns a script into a movie and why some movies grab hold of an audience and move them more than others. Beyond the screenplay and acting skills which are of course crucial is the visual artistry of the film. That is what we'll be looking at in this book in a brief, but thorough enough way to enlighten a beginner into the ways of movie making.

Another title for a cinematographer is a Director of Photography for the film. He or she manages the quality of the film, the lighting of a scene, etc and works very closely with the directors so as to successfully achieve the director's vision. But in addition to directors and cinematographers the actors, costume designers, effects artists, and many others involved in the making of a film often study how the film photography will be done so that what they bring to a scene compliments the frame as well. That is because everyone on set realizes that this is a visual medium and therefore the shots, angles, lighting and colors making up the scenes in a film are crucial to the effectiveness of relaying the movie's overall message.

As an example, imagine you're directing a scene where a young woman visits a small French village shortly after the end of World War II. All is gray and bleak except for her, a woman determined to help her people heal and rebuild. To emphasize the idea that she brings with her hope and determination you and the costume designer might place the woman in a bright, bold color to juxtapose her against her surroundings. If the shot of her is too close however it would miss much of the environment and her brightly colored dress would not have the emotional and visual impact desired. So the cinematographer might suggest that a long, high angle shot is used, using a drone high above in the air. Now the audience becomes like a bird or watchful angel, following the young woman as she walks slowly down the center of a rubble-strewn, war torn street in a bright, yellow dress signifying the peace and rebirth the town will experience by the end of the film.

From the above example it is clear just how essential it is for anyone seeking a career in film, or just seeking to appreciate films on a deeper level, to gain a basic understanding of the key visual elements used in filmmaking, why they are used and when. To help begin you on this journey this book focuses on the most commonly used shots and angles in films, as well as the basic tenets of lighting and color usage.

2

Chapter Two - Shots

The first segment we'll discuss are known as shots. Each scene in a film is made up of several shots which essentially describe the positioning of the camera when it captures the action taking place. In the next few segments we'll discuss not only what the practical uses are for the various basic shots, but how different shots relay specific messages and can convey emotions or other contextual themes.

- The Extreme Long Shot

This shot, as its name implies, is taken from a great distance and is typically used to establish the overall environment of the story. It sometimes is a panning shot which moves across horizontally, providing a panorama to the audience. Due the great distance this shot is typically taken outdoors and can be taken from as far as a quarter of a mile away. Certain films such as westerns or sci-fi fantasy films employ many such extreme long shots given the importance the characters' environments play in these films.

1977's *Star Wars*, directed by George Lucas, provided the audience not only with the visual wonder of outer space, but also contrasting images of a vast, sandy landscape in many scenes, bringing a raw and realistic environment to a science fiction story, something audiences did not expect. The broad long shots of this desert environment also show the similarities between the desolate expanse on land with the lonely expanse of space.

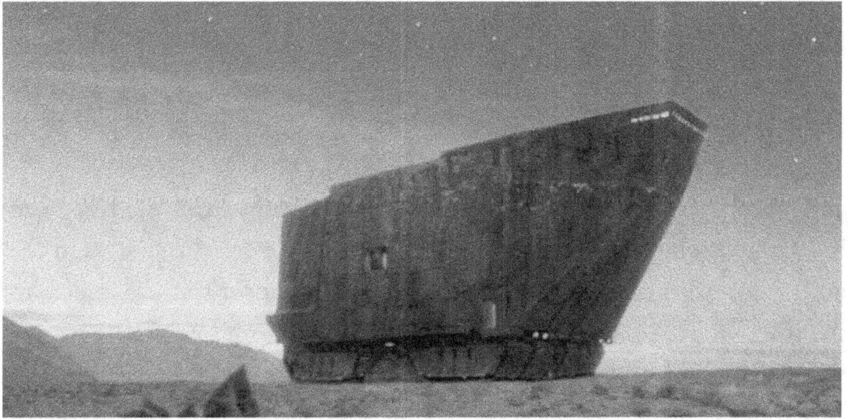

Star Wars (U.S.A. 1977), directed by George Lucas, cinematography by Gilbert Taylor.

With modern editing techniques and technologies such as drones, directors are able to make extreme long shots not as static as they once were. Some directors even start a shot at a great distance and slowly transition it ever closer and closer, guiding the audience further into the world of the characters.

One example of a modern technique with the extreme long shot is found in the beginning of Peter Jackson's *Lord of the Rings: The Two Towers*. Here the film begins with a sweeping panorama of a snow mountain range. The audience then begins to hear a low booming voice, seemingly coming from within the mountain. Through editing techniques the camera approaches the mountain side until it seems to effortlessly travel right through it, revealing the source of the voice. It is one of the main characters battling an ancient demon in the cavernous mine within the mountain. This is a great example of how the establishing, extreme long shot may be used in ever more dynamic ways to accentuate the emotion of a scene or grab hold of an audience and pull them into the story.

- Long (aka Wide) Shot

The name of this shot is a bit deceiving due to its origin being from live theater where the term "long" referred to the distance between the audience and the stage. Therefore, this shot is closer to the subjects in the frame than what one might expect, roughly representing what a live theatergoer would take in visually within the proscenium of a stage.

These shots are especially useful whenever it is necessary to show a character's full body. For instance in a fight scene there may be long shots to display the kicks and punches the characters exchange, alternated with closer shots showing the characters' anguished faces, such as in Martin Scorsese's masterpiece *Raging Bull,* where the shots of the boxing match scenes alternate between outside the ropes and within the ropes of the boxing ring, bringing the viewer deeper into the visceral reality of the main character.

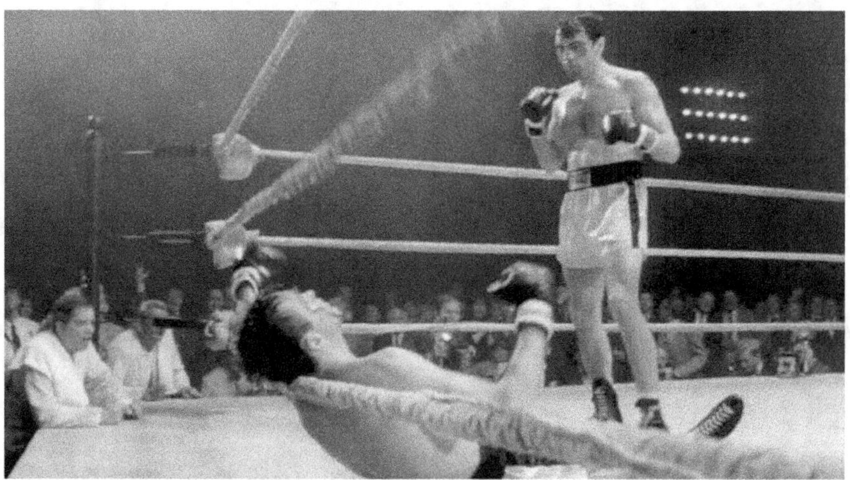

Raging Bull (U.S.A. 1980), directed by Martin Scorsese, cinematography by Michael Chapman.

Long shots are also very beneficial in movie musicals or any scene where the physical movements of the characters' bodies need to be seen in full. A director however may also use this shot when it seems to contradict the activity on screen as a way to express a unique emotion. For instance, in an intimate love scene a director may use a long shot to imply feelings of coldness or distance between the characters.

Within this category of the long shot is what is known as a full shot. This view is specifically far enough away to capture a subject's full form from head to toe, but close enough to allow the audience to still see even subtle facial expressions. These are superb shots for establishing the context of how a character interacts with the environment he or she is in and also for providing a detailed view of wardrobe, physical attributes, etc.

A great example of this is in *Forrest Gump* directed by Robert Zemeckis.

In the iconic full shots of Forrest sitting on a park bench the audience can view his slightly awkward and rigid physicality even while sitting alone in a beautiful, serene setting. Instantly the audience captures a sense of the character not quite fitting into his surroundings.

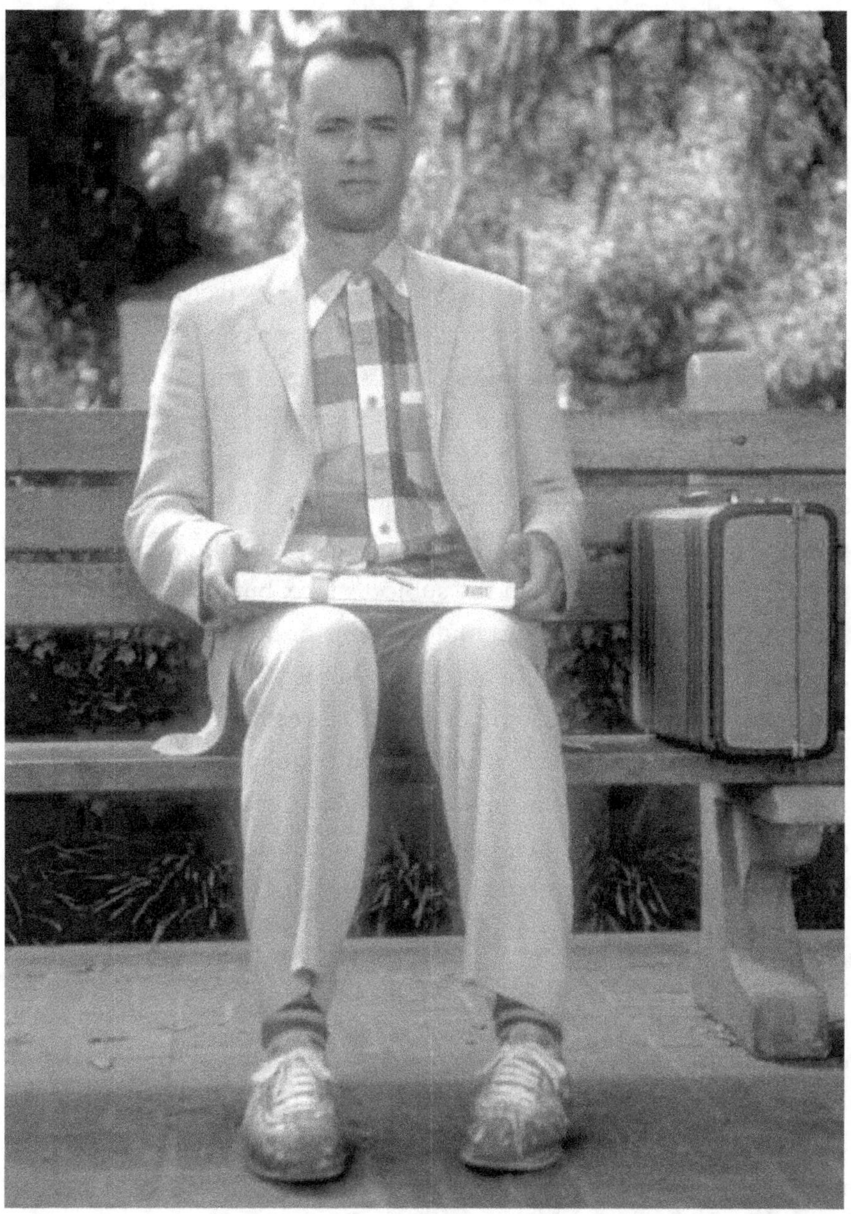

Forrest Gump (U.S.A. 1994), directed by Robert Zemeckis, cinematography by Don Burgess.

- Medium Shot

In the briefest of descriptions one could say that the medium shot is the top half of a full shot. But there are actually three distinct categories within the medium shot worth pointing out. The first is commonly called the *cowboy*, a reference to the fact that within the frame of this shot is the head down to just below the waist, perfect for allowing a clear view of a gun holster resting on the hip of a cowboy. If a scene's importance involves some physicality such as a gun or knife being drawn, or a punch being pulled, then this is the ideal shot to use.

Similar to the *cowboy*, but slightly zoomed in to just show a subject's waist up to the top of the head is known simply as a *medium shot*. Here you see even more detail on the subject's face, but still can view any important physicality, background elements or other characters in the scene. This is a crucial shot where the subject's reaction may be in response to something occurring which the director wants the audience to view as well. Alternatively however a director may purposely want the audience to solely focus on the main subject of the shot and not any other elements or characters. In this case the *medium close-up shot* would be best as it provides a full picture of a character's head and shoulders and much less of the surroundings.

A great use of the medium shot is in Steven Spielberg's *Indiana Jones and the Raiders of the Lost Ark* where the audience anxiously watches as Indiana Jones carefully attempts to swipe a golden idol from its pedestal and replace it with an equally weighted bag of sand. The viewer here needs to clearly see the full operation at hand, but Spielberg wants the viewer to also experience Jones's intense concentration. We grow just as nervous as Jones does as he tries to best calculate how much sand must be in the bag and we hold our breath along with him as he deftly does the swap, panicking as we realize it doesn't work.

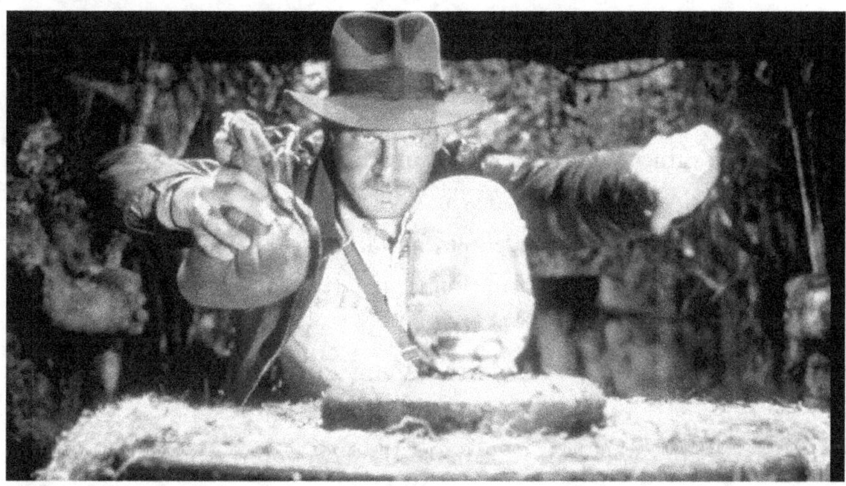

Indiana Jones and the Raiders of the Lost Ark (U.S.A. 1981), directed by Steven Spielberg, cinematography by Douglas Slocombe.

- The Close-Up

When a director or cinematographer wants to focus solely on the character and his or her emotions or reactions often a close-up shot is used, which essentially is just a shot of the subject's face. No other surroundings are typically visible to the audience. In some cases cinematographer may zoom in even further to just the eyes, mouth, etc which is what is termed an Extreme Close-up. These Extreme Close-Ups are often found in more formalist, artistic films or in a scene where the director really wants to symbolize an overpowering emotion such as fear or desire.

One effective use of the close-up is found in horror and suspense films. In these genres audiences typically are first lulled into a sense of security with long shots revealing a great deal of the surrounding environment. From this vantage point viewers presume they'll be able to clearly see any danger approaching. To ramp up the tension and excitement the director will then suddenly pull in close, perhaps just showing the subject character's face or even the back of the head. This is greatly unsettling to the viewer who now feels the subject's same level of vulnerability. Think of the scene in *The Silence of the Lambs*, directed by Jonathan Demme, where from the perspective of the killer the camera closes in on the back of Clarice's head as she nervously makes her way through a dark house, terrified in the knowledge that the villain is in the house with her. Neither she nor the audience know what will happen as she makes her way from room to room. When the audience finally sees the hand of the villain reach towards Clarice's hair we jump and feel helpless that we can't warn her. Eliciting the sensations of fear in an audience is precisely what these genres of horror and suspense must achieve to be successful and the judicious use of camera shots is crucial to achieving that emotional response from the viewers.

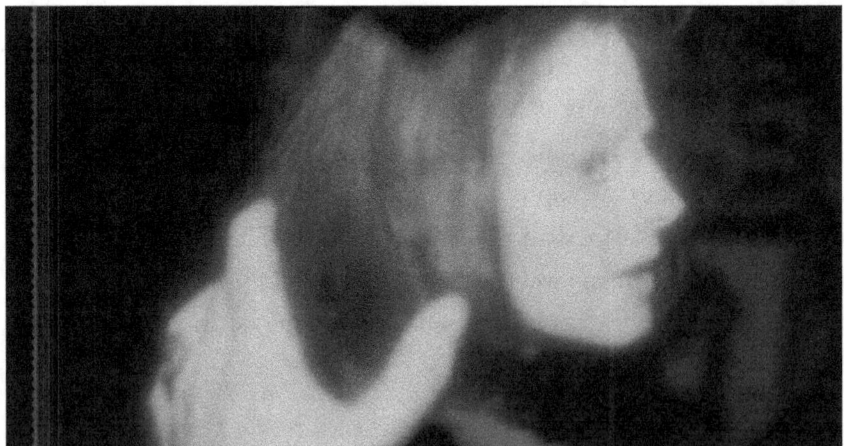

The Silence of the Lambs (U.S.A. 1991), directed by Jonathan Demme, cinematography by Tak Fujimoto.

3

Chapter Three: Angles

The next segment we'll review is the angle used in a shot or series of shots. The angle is simply defined as the positioning of the camera relative to the subject, rather than the distance or location of the camera from the subject. In addition to the type of shot used, the angle of a shot is just as important to the scene and can either subtly affect the scene's messaging with a slight tilt or express very powerful emotions and messages through extreme angles.

- Eye-level angle

The traditional angle, one used by realistic film makers, often in documentaries or other films grounded in realism, is the eye-level angle. This angle is typically level with the horizon, approximately five or six feet off the ground. Such shots are excellent for what is sometimes called the master shot, which establishes a scene and the environment of the characters. These shots aren't in themselves dramatic given their realistic perspective, but the choice of this shot in certain circumstances can actually make a strong impact on the audience. An effective use of the eye-level angle for dramatic purposes is where the director wants the audience to feel they are participating in the action of the scene alongside the characters. For instance the scene may be a prison yard and the use of an eye-level angle at a medium shot distance from the prisoners in the scene may make the viewer feel like they themselves are one of the prisoners, being lined up and ushered by guards back to their cells. A similar scene may be a wartime scenario where eye-level, close distance shots are also used to bring the audience into the action, making them more viscerally aware of the horrors and dangers of the battlefield.

In *The Deer Hunter*, directed by Oliver Stone, the majority of the film appears at eye-level, yet this film certainly delivers a strong emotional impact. By presenting scenes of terror and desperation with the same lens, level and distance as those of weddings and small-town everyday experiences, Stone emphasizes how real and tangible both worlds are in the lives of the men returning from Vietnam, and how difficult it is for them to deal with the traumatic experiences that have forever changed them.

- The High Angle

Looking down on someone is a common phrase used to describe the attitude of superiority, control and condescension. So what better way to express a character's sense of powerlessness, subjugation or inferiority than having the camera literally look down on them? This is exactly what the high angle accomplishes. To achieve this typically the camera must be placed either on a crane or some other high point relative to the characters, unless perhaps the characters themselves are sitting or lying on the ground below the level of the camera. The distance from the camera to the subject may vary depending on the preference of the director and what effect he or she is trying to achieve, but most often the distance is in the medium shot range, allowing for a clear view of the character's facial expressions in the scene. The perspective too may be representative of another character looking down on them or the angle may simply signify the current emotional state of the characters.

In Frank Darabont's *The Shawshank Redemption* the main character Andy Dufresne stands in the rain, looking up to the sky with arms outstretched as if to seek God's forgiveness and to cleanse away his sins. Here the use of a high angle helps accentuate his humility and repentance in a way an eye-level angle would not have accomplished as effectively.

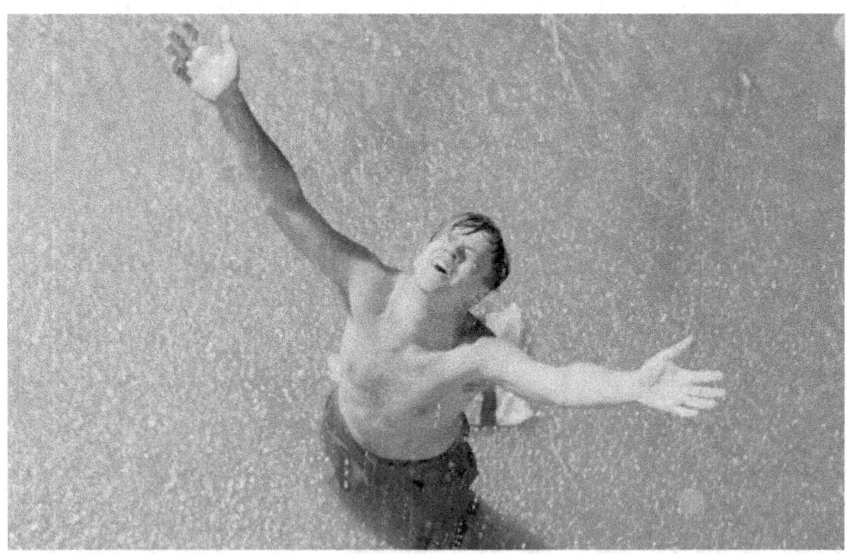

The Shawshank Redemption (U.S.A. 1994), directed by Frank Darabont, cinematography by Roger Deakins.

- Birds-eye view

The birds-eye view angle is a type of aerial shot that can either be from a somewhat high vantage point or just a few feet above the characters' heads, and it is typically directly above the characters. For this reason the angle is sometimes referred to as an overhead shot. Since this shot is typically at a 90 degree angle above the subjects in a frame, directors use it sparingly due to it being an unrealistic way for audiences to view the world. When employed it can disorient an audience and potentially alienate them, pulling them out of the film, however when used effectively it can have a dramatic symbolic effect. Some of the emotions this angle can help accentuate are those of claustrophobia, entrapment, foreboding and the feeling of being continually watched. It can also be used as a way to emphasize the juxtaposition of characters against their surroundings.

Brian De Palma, in his film *The Untouchables*, masterfully uses the overhead shot, throughout this film. In these scenes where this angle is used we often see men, typically the mobsters under the control of Al Capone. From directly above their forms are lost so while in life they may each be large, intimidating men, from above they appear diminutive and weak as compared to the surrounding environment. In one scene we see a man who had fallen from a building and is now lying lifeless on top of a car. Identical cars are in a row next to it and many faceless men are in the street watching in shock, each appearing in similar clothing as the dead body. This perspective emphasizes the vulnerability of the men in this mafia world where the wrong step could lead to death. De Palma uses this technique again with the same intention when he places the camera directly above a large white table, at which are seated several mobsters. First, from a low angle we watch nervously as Al Capone circles around the men, towering above them as he speaks. He then bludgeons one of them to death with a baseball bat and the camera angle shifts instantly to a birds-eye view to watch motionlessly, along with the men around the table, as the blood slowly trickles across the white table cloth. Again, the birds-eye view captures just how powerless these men are under the constant eye of the ruthless Capone.

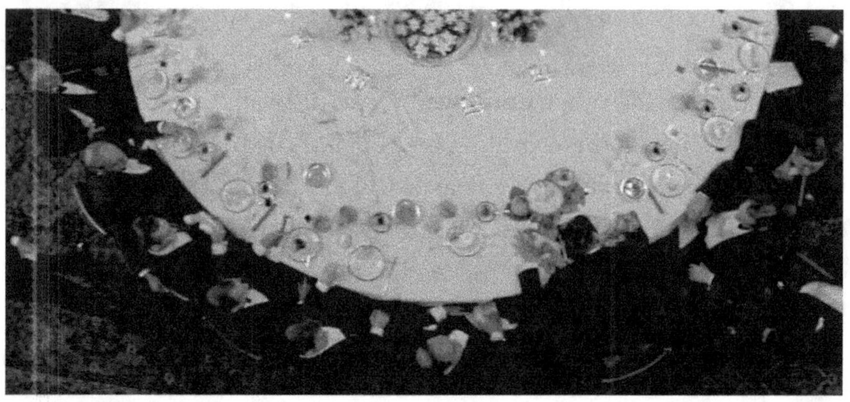

The Untouchables (U.S.A. 1987), directed by Brian De Palma, cinematography by Stephen H. Burum.

- Low Angle

As alluded to briefly above, a low angle shot is often helpful in accentuating a subject's superiority, thereby having an opposite effect as the high angle shot. With the camera now pointing upwards towards the subject, the character appears more dominant, powerful. There is also typically little else in the shot other than perhaps the sky given the camera's point of view.

Now there can be practical purposes for a lower angle shot, such as making an actor look taller, but these angles are primarily used for expressive and symbolic purposes. In horror movies a low angle of the villain certainly accentuates the danger, making the villain even more threatening and scary. Directors may also employ this angle to symbolically reveal a temporary moment of strength felt by a character.

In *American Beauty*, directed by Sam Mendes, the young teenage boy Ricky is a quiet, somewhat withdrawn teen dealing with an overbearing father whose strict personality is in direct contrast to Ricky's gentle, introspective nature. Often feeling lost and overwhelmed by his environment, his one outlet that gives him peace and inner confidence is his video camera. Being behind a veil of safety looking through the lens of his camera Ricky feels free to observe life and piece together a sense of meaning from it. As Ricky is filming, Mendes selects a unique low-angle shot, almost from the ground, looking up at Ricky. Behind him is a peaceful blue sky with clouds and Ricky's figure is large, almost distorted. The audience can sense his isolation, but also an inner strength in Ricky as it seems that it is in these moments Ricky feels most confident and in control.

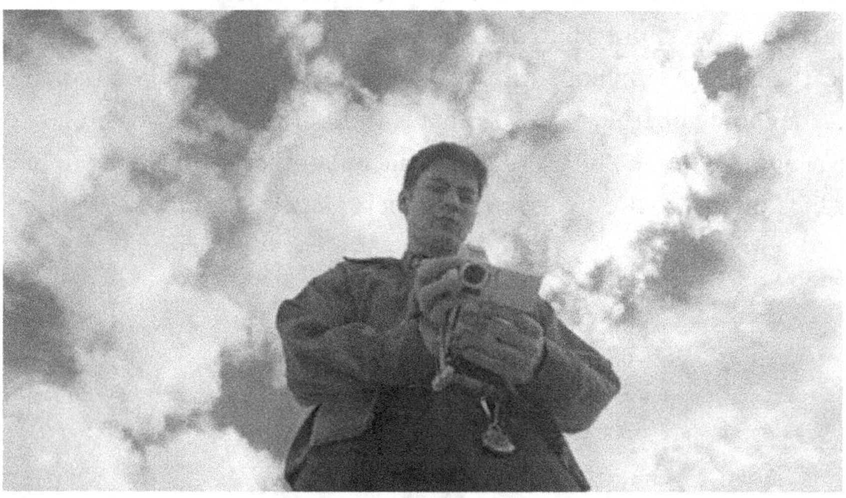

American Beauty (U.S.A. 1999), directed by Sam Mendes, cinematography by Conrad L. Hall.

- Oblique Angle

When a director wants to induce a strong level of anxiety in the audience, perhaps even purposely disorienting and disarming them to match the feeling of uneasiness amongst the characters in a film, he or she may employ the use of an oblique angle, also sometimes referred to as a Dutch angle. This angle is when the camera is tilted laterally, not just up or down as in the high and low angles. What this does is skew the horizon so that the view is no longer level. The effect is that it sometimes makes the characters in the shot look as though they are about to fall down.

A very effective use of the oblique angle is in fight scenes as the audience's sense of precariousness is amplified. In horror or superhero movies often villains will be filmed at an oblique angle, perhaps coupled with a low angle vantage point. This emphasizes not only the villain's seeming invincibility, but also the disorder and disruption they bring to their environments. Another purpose for using oblique angles throughout superhero films is that they not only create tension, but pay homage to the artistry of the comic books they are bringing to life, which often also drew each comic panel at an oblique angle.

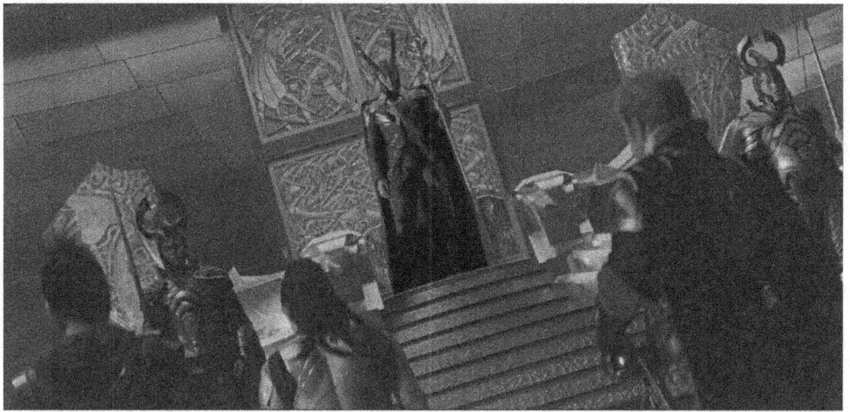

Thor (U.S.A. 2011), directed by Kenneth Branagh, cinematography by Haris Zambarloukos.

Another very common usage of the oblique angle is when the subject is either drunk, drugged or going mad and the director wants to simulate the feeling of unsteadiness for the audience. Terry Gilliam uses oblique angles frequently throughout his film *12 Monkeys*, especially in the asylum scenes, to evoke the sensations of disorientation and confusion, as well as the effects of drugs the main character is experiencing.

The most interesting aspect however of the oblique angle is its origin, which is rooted in the expressionist movement in Germany during World War I. During this time Germany banned the import of foreign films and so German filmmakers had to look to visual art, not Hollywood, for inspiration and guidance. What the expressionist artists were capturing in their paintings were bold and unnerving expressions of the world around them, often with figures and buildings,etc contorted and misshapen. Directors during that time, such as Robert Wiener, were enticed by distorted angles and perspectives in this art and brought it to the screen. Wiener's famous film, *The Cabinet of Dr. Caligari*, released in 1920, was a ground-breaking film that influenced filmmakers around the world and still does. In this film the sets themselves were built at skewed angles, whereas most contemporary directors now such as Gilliam simply tilt the camera's angle to achieve similar results.

4

Chapter Four: Light and Dark

While the lighting of a photograph is understandably complex one doesn't sometimes appreciate the advantages still photographers have over cinematographers. First and foremost, a still photographer has a dark room wherein the choice of paper, the choice of development and filters, etc are at his or her disposal. In the dynamic environment of a film each movement by an actor or object can affect where the light hits, as can the texture and shape of items within the frame. Yet even with these disadvantages lighting in films is usually very intentional as it can so effectively convey emotions and other meanings.

Since the beginnings of poetry we have always associated emotions like sadness and danger with darkness and emotions of joy, happiness and security with light. These tenets are well embedded in the core ways in which light is used in film. The terminology used when there is a lot of light and very little contrast or shadow is known as *'high key'* and is the typical choice for genres such as comedies and musicals. Here, even the moments of conflict are not weighed down by contrasted lighting, sending a subtle message to the audience that whatever has gone somewhat awry will soon correct itself.

Where directors elect to light their scenes in 'high contrast' are when the film is perhaps a tragedy or drama. Here the sharp, defined shadows relay the severity of the situations the characters find themselves in as well as the ideas of navigating between evil and good, truth and deception. The *film noir* films of the 1950's were popular for using these high contrast lighting techniques.

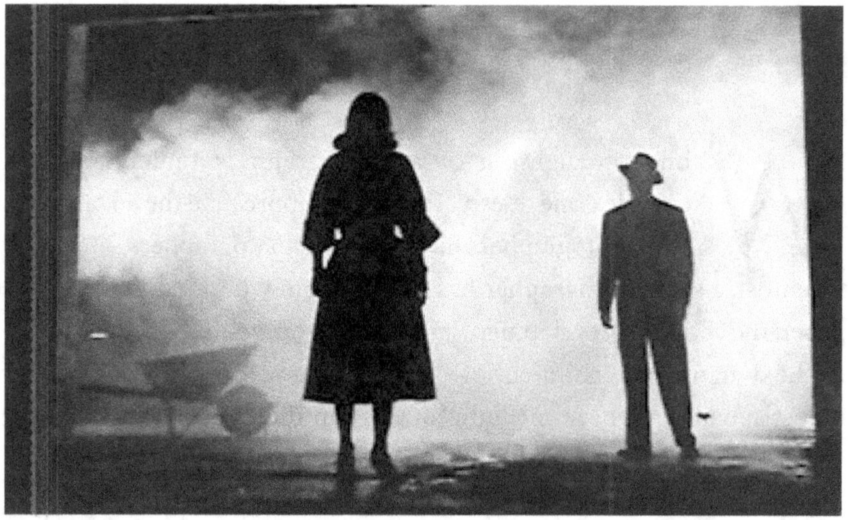

The Big Combo (U.S.A., 1955), directed by Joseph H. Lewis, cinematography by John Alton.

Some directors of genres such as mysteries or supernatural thrillers may also light scenes in *'low key'* where shadows may be diffused and ghostly pools of light fill the frame. Finally, when seeking a highly realistic, almost documentary-like feel to a film many cinematographers will dispense with the use of lamps, reflectors, etc and rely solely on natural lighting. In Barry Jenkins' *Moonlight*, most scenes are bathed in whatever natural light sources exist in the environment of the characters, bringing a raw view that draws the audience into the realistic struggles of the main character.

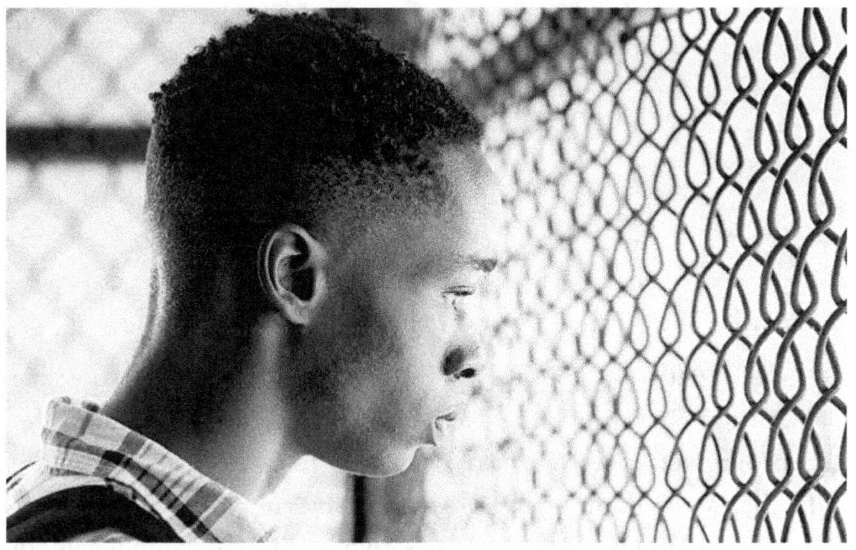

Moonlight (U.S.A. 2016), directed by Barry Jenkins, cinematography by James Laxton.

In addition to the degree of light itself directors can also achieve dramatic results in where the light is placed and how it reflects against an object. From the somewhat obvious light on a face from below making it look sinister and foreboding to subtle backlighting which can provide a halo effect on the characters in a frame, there are countless ways to employ lighting techniques to further convey the director's intent for a scene.

$$5$$

Chapter Five: Color

In the 1940's the ability to make films in color was finally possible and slowly through the decades as the technology of color film progressed directors have been able to utilize this tool more to further assist them in creating a cohesive, impactful work of art on screen, in much the same way as colors are used symbolically in paintings and novels. Orson Welles even was quoted as saying 'A film is never really good unless the camera is an eye in the head of a poet" and so it is no wonder that as color film technology has now become more advanced directors are fully exploring the poetic impact of color in their films. We see color being used in subtle ways such as the use of a colored filter so that the whole scene is either amplified or muted to convey a specific emotion. Alternatively, the director may select a specific bold color for a main character's costume while keeping all other objects and characters in a similar color scheme. This is done as a way to draw attention to the main subject and convey a specific emotion or message to the audience.

In general, the use of color tends to be a somewhat inconspicuous element, with the overt uses being done sparingly in a film for a more obvious effect. A great example of the subtle usage of color is in Ridley Scott's *Blade Runner*. All but the final scene in the film take place at night, often in the rain, with the only real vibrant colors coming from the many neon signs piercing through the rain or reflected on the wet pavement. The lighting in many scenes harkens back to *film noir* with its high contrast shadows, but the coloring of scenes range from symbolizing the fake, unsympathetic futuristic world in which the characters must survive to very subtle, soft lighting during the fleeting romantic moments.

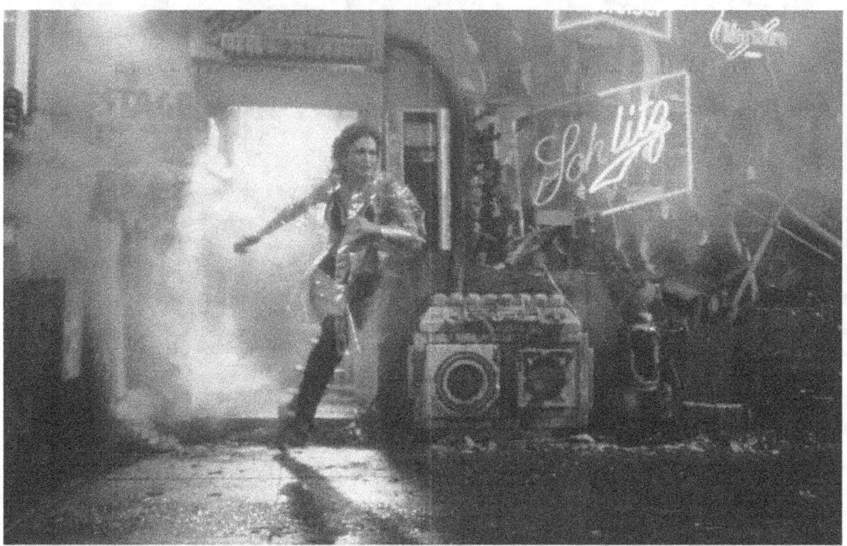

Blade Runner (U.S.A. 1982), directed by Ridley Scott, cinematography by Jordan Cronenweth

An example of a more overt use of color is in Steven Spielburg's *Schindler's List*. The film is entirely in black and white until we see a scene where a little girl walks through a busy crowd of people wearing a muted red coat. The color red, being the color of blood, is often associated with danger and death, and that definitely comes to mind when considering the subject matter of the film being about the plight of Jews during World War II. But boldly placing a color on the little girl's coat where all else is black and gray seems to more signify a defiance and a strength still present among the Jewish people. This child therefore represents a hope for survival and rebirth.

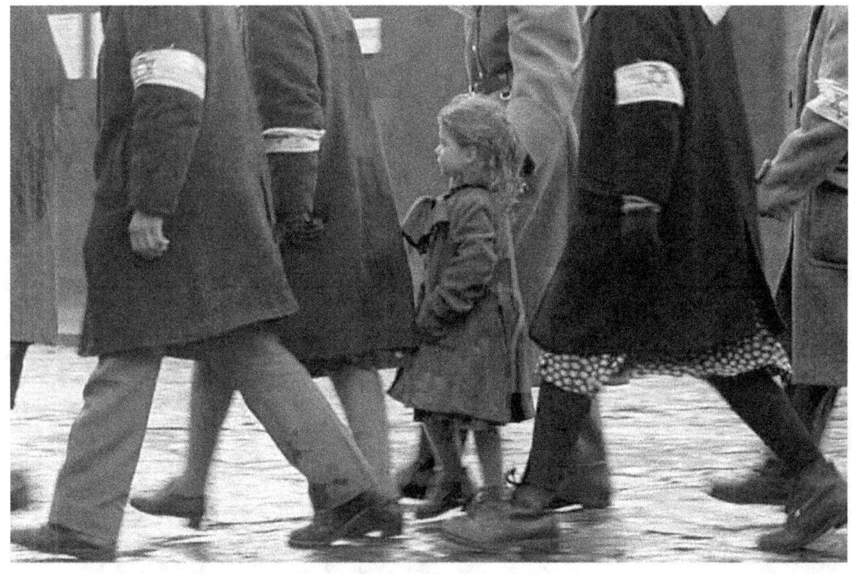

Schindler's List (U.S.A. 1993), directed by Steven Spielberg, cinematography by Janusz Kaminski.

6

Chapter Six - Conclusion

The film photography elements such as shots, angles, lighting and color discussed throughout this book really comprise the essential building blocks of cinematography. Since each scene is made up of several shots the director can relay a multitude of emotions, states of being, etc through the effective use of these tools to arrive at a film that doesn't just tell a story, but brings that story to life and hopefully forges an intimate connection with the audience.

So whether you are just wanting to better appreciate a movie you're watching or are seeking to break into the business and make a film of your own you now have a basic understanding of the essential elements of film photography - the shots, angles, lighting and color in films.

I hope you enjoyed this brief introduction into what is a hugely complex, but gratifying artistic endeavor - the making of a film. If you did enjoy this book please consider leaving a review on Amazon and let me know what other aspects of film making you might be interested in learning about.

7

Resources

Resources

Giannetti. (1996). *Understanding Movies* (7th ed.). Prentice Hall.

Mascelli. (2005). *The Five C's of Cinematography: Motion Picture Filming Techniques* (1st ed.). Silman-James Press.

DeGuzman, K. (2021, June 18). *What is a Full Shot in Film? Types of Shots in Film Explained*. StudioBinder. https://www.studiobinder.com/blog/what-is-a-full-shot-in-film-definition/

Aton, L. E. (2021, August 3). *73 of the Best Quotes About Filmmaking*. Film Crux. https://www.filmcrux.com/blog/best-filmmaking-quotes

Jackson, P. (Director). (2002) *The Lord of the Rings: The Two Towers* [Film]. New Line Cinema.

Cimino, M. (Director). (1978) *The Deer Hunter* [Film]. EMI.

RESOURCES

Lucas, G. (Director). (1977) *Star Wars* [Film]. 20th Century Fox. Still capture under Fair Use.

Scorsese, M. (Director). (1980) *Raging Bull* [Film]. Chartoff-Winkler. Still capture under Fair Use.

Zemeckis, R. (Director). (1994) *Forrest Gump* [Film]. The Tisch Company. Still capture under Fair Use.

Spielberg, S. (Director) (1981) *Indiana Jones and the Raiders of the Lost Ark* [Film]. The Walt Disney Company, Lucasfilm, Ltd. Still capture under Fair Use.

Demme, J. (Director) (1991) *The Silence of the Lambs* [Film]. Strong Heart Productions. Still capture under Fair Use.

Darabont, F. (Director) (1994) *The Shawshank Redemption* [Film]. Castle Rock Entertainment. Still capture under Fair Use.

DePalma, B. (Director) (1987) *The Untouchables* [Film]. Art Linson, Paramount. Still capture under Fair Use.

Mendes, S. (Director) (1999) *American Beauty* [Film]. Dreamworks. Still capture under Fair Use.

Branagh, K. (Director) (2011) *Thor* [Film]. Marvel Studios. Still capture under Fair Use.

Lewis, J.H. (Director) (1955) *The Big Combo* [Film]. Theodora and Security. Still capture under Fair Use.

Scott, Ridley (Director) (1982) *Blade Runner* [Film]. The Ladd Company, Shaw Brothers, Warner Bros. and Blade Runner Partnership. Still capture under Fair Use.

Spielberg, S. (Director) (1993) *Schindler's List* [Film]. Steven Spielberg, Universal Pictures, Amblin Entertainment. Still capture under Fair Use.

Gilliam, T. (Director) (1995) *12 Monkeys* [Film]. Universal Pictures. Still capture under Fair Use.

Jenkins, B. (Director) (2016) *Moonlight* [Film]. Adele Romanski, Dede Gardner, Jeremy Kleinger. Still capture under Fair Use.